Contemporary Follies

Keith Moskow & Robert Linn

Introduction / **Marc Kristal**

The Monacelli Press

Introduction / **Marc Kristal**

An architectural folly of the sort that reached its apogee in the eighteenth and nineteenth centuries, primarily in the British Isles and throughout Europe and North America, is generally defined as an ornamental structure intended to decorate or enhance a garden or landscape. As the name implies, such buildings were typically fanciful or exotic in design, and they often took the form of classical temples, medieval castles or towers, Egyptian pyramids, and ancient ruins. As the name, which derives from the French folie ("madness"), also suggests, follies were frequently considered to be expressions of ego, eccentricity, or foolishness: expensive, isolated objects built to gratify the whims of their creators.

In actual fact, the folly of yore was a more complex, various creation. Most were to one or another degree habitable, functioning as observatories, retreats, libraries, and places to entertain; indeed, the UK-based Landmark Trust, a building preservation charity, has restored multiple well-known follies, among them Beckford's Tower (Bath, 1827), Clavell Tower (Dorset, 1830) and The Ruin (North Yorkshire, 1767), and rents them out to history-minded vacationers. In some instances, a folly's design peculiarities were related to its use. Dunmore, Scotland's famous eighteenth-century Pineapple, a linear pavilion topped by a magnificently sculpted, pineapple-shaped stone cupola, served as a hothouse in which the fruit was grown; the design of the Wonderful Barn (Kildare, Ireland, 1743), which resembles an upside-down ice cream cone, suited its function as a granary. The fact that follies were usually small scale with uncomplicated programs — in a sense, glorified maquettes — also encouraged a degree of aesthetic perfection that might otherwise have been unachievable. Sir William Chambers's diminutive eighteenth-century Casino at Marino in Dublin, to cite an example, is regarded as the finest neoclassical structure in Ireland.

Although follies could be derided for their idiosyncrasy, this is also their great appeal. Follies remain most interesting as expressions of emotion and belief, personal philosophy, and individual sensibility. Clytha Castle (Abergavenny, Scotland, 1792) was a memorial to a departed loved one ("undertaken with the purpose of relieving a mind afflicted by the loss of a most excellent wife," reads its dedication); the late sixteen-century Triangular Lodge, near Rushton, England, was an affirmation, in architecture, of its creator's Roman Catholicism. The writer and folly-phile Gwyn Headley's observation that "a folly is a state of mind" was eloquently demonstrated, in the early twentieth century, by Antonio Gaudí's fantastical Park Güell in Barcelona, and again, decades later, by the Watts Towers in Los Angeles, the thirty-three-year-long visionary effort of an immigrant laborer named Simon Rodia. That they were meant to be fun is noted by the Folly Fellowship, a English preservation organization, which states that follies "were built for pleasure before purpose."

That they were just as often used as memento mori can be seen at the late eighteenth-century French landscape garden Désert de Retz, home to the colonne brisée, a summer house taking the form of a gigantic ruined classical column—a reminder that all existence, no matter how exalted, remains transitory.

Above all, while the typical folly stood as an isolated moment on the landscape—in nature but pointedly not of it—such structures, by virtue of their very apartness, could not help but provoke an inquiry into humankind's position in the natural world. The garden, a place restorative, consoling, and pleasurable, ideal for the contemplation of life's beauty and the inevitability of its end: How do we find our proper place here? each folly seems to ask. What is our role, and where do we belong?

Keith Moskow and Robert Linn's present-day curiosity about how small structures can affect our relationship to nature—what the architects call "rural interventions"—grew out of a larger, longstanding inquiry into the manner in which modest design gambits can have a transformative effect on a given situation. The landscape on which they initially pursued their interest was urban, via pocket-sized projects, set largely in Boston and designed to have a positive impact on metropolitan living. "We created smoking kiosks called 'Urban Hookahs' that attached to streetlight poles after Boston instituted a no-smoking ban, and we found ways to stack cars in leftover slots of space," Linn recalls, drawing on the firm's "urban interventions" portfolio. "It was really about how to make the city more delightful with small design moves." Having tackled the challenge from an urbanistic standpoint, Moskow and Linn then began to think about it, so to speak, ruralistically. The idea, Moskow explains, was "to make the experience of being in a rural environment more accessible, to create projects that allow you to experience the natural landscape in a transformative way." This led them, eventually, to the idea of the contemporary folly: a structure that—in contravention of the typology's original iteration— engaged with nature rather than serving as a detached decorative moment, and that encouraged contemplation of our surroundings, not through separation, but by altering the ways in which we perceive them.

Accordingly, each of the fifty-one projects selected by the architects for this book in some way addresses the relationship between the individual and the natural world—how we experience it, inhabit it, make it a part of our personal cosmography, how we give to it and take from it. Whereas the follies of the past tended to be elaborate architectural creations that strove for a transcendental excellence, a surprising number of Moskow and Linn's selections (though most assuredly not all of them) reveal themselves to be sketches, ideas quickly worked out and simply constructed, oftentimes by students. Yet like the studies artists make for larger, more "important" works, wherein motifs are explored simply to see where they will lead, these small-scale projects have a vitalizing, illuminating immediacy. In their description of the Moore Honey House, a beekeeping structure in Cashiers, North Carolina, the architects describe "the tense interplay between the beekeeper's equipment and the bee's willingness to adapt to it." To a remarkable degree, that charged, critical nexus—the point at which humankind meets nature, and something takes place—defines the contemporary folly.

To be sure, certain of Moskow and Linn's selections— Heatherwick Studio's science fiction–influenced

Sitooterie II and the skating shelters, designed by Patkau Architects, that resemble a cluster of abstract penguins huddled on a frozen river — appear as follies in the old sense; still others, like their historical predecessors, serve as overlooks, retreats, and places for meditation or self-expression. Yet even within categories that conform to precedent, the differences between then and now are telling. As such observatories as Austria's Top of Tyrol and Aurland Lookout in Norway demonstrate, advances in architecture and engineering can intensify our experience of the natural world in previously unachievable ways, expanding the folly's potential and transforming the traditional, paradoxically inward-looking "ivory tower" into a more dramatic, embracing experience. And whereas early follies typically bore little or no relationship to their surroundings, their present-day successors are pointedly, sometimes exquisitely,

attuned to place. Moorhead & Moorhead's Mobile Chaplet, a movable chapel based in Fargo, North Dakota, resembles the Conestoga wagons that settled the plains, invokes the nineteenth-century itinerant preacher ever in search of savable souls, and features a lightly woven canopy as sensitive to the breeze as a wheat field. In every way does the Chaplet reference, and feel a part of, its region — but put it in Connecticut, and it would be a folly.

The authors have grouped their selections into six categories, but a journey through the book reveals that much of what is here defies ready classification. If there is a unifying perception, it is perhaps the rich variety of ways in which the built and natural environments can beneficially intercommunicate. Some projects do so very directly, by drawing on local craft traditions and materials and a design/build ethos, and allowing existing cultural, ecological, and geographical conditions to give form to an idea. Others, including two sculptural bat houses, use design to make a component of nature — in this case, the brown bat — less fearsome and more appreciable as a part of a well-functioning ecosystem. The Pinohuacho Observation Deck, in a region of Chile transitioning from a farming and logging economy into an agro-tourism zone, demonstrates how the reassuring presence of contemporary design can serve, in nature, as an aesthetic cue, signaling that an area has been "re-branded" and is available for enjoyment. Many of the objects designed to shelter people from nature's depredations—even ones as stridently "un-natural" as Ply Architecture's Shadow Pavilion—simultaneously heighten awareness of their surroundings, by intensifying the effects of light, sound, aroma, and weather. There are even structures, notably Michael Van Valkenburgh's Ice Garden on Martha's Vineyard, that celebrate nature by recontextualizing it within the artifice of architecture—thereby demonstrating that people can enjoy, and even contribute to, a rural landscape while still speaking our individual, all too human, language.

All of the works have their merits. But if there is one that seems most perfectly to crystallize the authors' intent, it is Shedding Light, a public art project by Erika Zekos in Amherst, Massachusetts. The idea is simplicity itself: Zekos found an anonymous vernacular building—a 150-year-old tobacco barn, sited in the middle of an empty field—filled it with powerful lights, opened its ventilation panels, and flipped the switch. Yet by converting a quotidian object into an architectural lantern of startling impact, the artist transformed it into a significant artifact of aesthetic and cultural history, one that provokes a reconsideration of the surrounding landscape and, indeed, the entire region as development expunges its architectural past. It is the smallest of rural interventions—yet the gesture powerfully reorders our perceptions.

Whether our circumstances are urban or rural, familiarity makes us blind; it deprives us of the delight to be derived from the unexpected moment that—like Shedding Light—delivers illumination. The follies of the past were known colloquially as "eye-catchers" because they did just that: compelled their beholders to stop, look, and discover anew the incomparable eloquence of the natural world. With Contemporary Follies, Moskow and Linn have done as much for our own time by giving us fifty-one sublime opportunities to open our eyes.

PLATFORMS, TOWERS, AND LOOKOUTS OPEN ONTO SPECTACULAR NATURAL PANORAMAS.   **OBSERVATION**

Top of Tyrol

LAAC ARCHITECTS / STUBAI GLACIER, AUSTRIA

This observation platform at the center of the Stubai Glacier offers an unobstructed 360-degree view of the Tyrolean Alps, from Zillertal to the Dolomites. To reach the platform, visitors must take a train, then the funicular, a set of steps, and a final 70-meter walk through the landscape.

Top of Tyrol was commissioned by one of Austria's glacier ski authorities with the aim of encouraging more tourism to the area. The clients wanted to create a spiritual place in which even stressed mountaineers can find peace and recuperate while letting their thoughts wander and enjoy the seemingly endless expanses of the mountain world.

Creating an uninvasive element in this rugged natural landscape required a structure that was both delicate and incredibly strong. Construction had to be done exclusively by helicopter so there was a high level of prefabrication; simple mounting surfaces and accuracy of fit are essential criteria for building in the high alpine permafrost.

The platform is made of weather-resistant steel; the twisted swords are box-section beams of Corten steel. Rock anchors and reinforced concrete brace the foundations. This balancing act of engineering and architecture achieves a poetic lightness, as steel, concrete, and wood seem only incidental to the floating platform.

Visible from afar, the Jueberg lookout tower is prominently positioned at the end of a long flight of stairs, marking the limit of the city and the transition to landscape. The tower is a new landmark, an attraction for the regional garden and flower festival Landesgartenschau Hemer 2010, and for the region of Southern North Rhine-Westphalia.

The structure is based on the principle of the hyperboloid, which was introduced by the engineer Vladimir G. Shukhov. It consists of 240 straight timber members of glued and laminated Siberian larch woven into a double layer of lattice. The outer, delicate member system bears the loads; additional vertical members, such as steel columns or a center mast, were purposely omitted. Steel needles anchor the construction up to six meters deep in the bedrock.

The rigidity of the tower is reduced gradually from the foundation to the top by decreasing the number of timber rods and opening the lattice as loads diminish. Six supports in the lowest plane are

reduced to five in the next level, then four, three, and finally, two rods. This allows for an increasing panoramic view during the climb to the observation deck.

Corresponding to the forest aisle, the foot of the tower has been kept slim, with a diameter of about six meters. Inside the structure, five flights of winding steel stairs lead to the observation deck, which offers a spectacular 360-degree view.

Jueberg Tower

BIRK AND HEILMEYER ARCHITECTS
HEMER, GERMANY

SplitFrame is a wildlife-viewing structure designed and constructed to maximize environmental exposure while minimizing impact. Two integral pieces, a floating observation deck and an elevated viewing station, are connected by a hinged staircase, allowing the deck to rise and fall with the seasonal change in water levels. The project is situated at the end of a long berm, a vestige of the site's former use as a commercial cranberry bog, which has been integrated into the project as a path drawing visitors out over the water.

SplitFrame

NORTH STUDIO AT WESLEYAN UNIVERSITY
HELEN CARLSON WILDLIFE SANCTUARY, PORTLAND, CONNECTICUT

Helsinki Zoo Lookout Tower

AVANTO ARCHITECTS / HELSINKI, FINLAND

This lookout tower is located on Korkeasaari Island. The site is eighteen meters above sea level, and the tower is very visible from Helsinki. The natural setting inspired the free form of the tower; it follows the surrounding stonewall and skirts around a group of birches.

The structure behaves like an eggshell; even when the grid shell, which consists of more than 600 joints, is punctured, it withstands the load. The load-bearing structure consists of 72 long battens that were bent and twisted on site in the shape of seven individual forms.

The curved form challenges Western culture, which favors rectangular forms. The box is considered a standard shape. In nature, however, curvilinear forms are omnipresent. Curvilinear forms are also closer to the human physique than rectilinear ones, which explains why people may experience organic forms in human terms.

This large wooden cube is in the mountains, in an isolated area that was devastated by the Villarrica volcano in 1971. Twelve kilometers from the nearest road and sixteen from the nearest village, the site is accessible only on foot.

The observation deck is a resting spot for hikers in this remote area. It is also a visible symbol of the region's attempts to develop agro-tourism in the wake of a volcanic eruption that upset local farming traditions and forced the relocation of many villagers. With the reconditioning of old logging

Pinohuacho
Observation Deck

roads for horseback riding and trekking, the observation tower will become the nexus of the traditional, if impoverished, past and the possibilities of a more secure future as it welcomes tourists.

Making reference to the forestry and furniture-making traditions of the area, the designers constructed a giant wooden cube that is open on two of the vertical sides. A simple thick board cantilevered from the wall forms a bench for sitting and contemplating the view. Outside, cantilevered steps climb to the roof where visitors can get longer

views. Abandoned Coigue wood was used so no trees were cut down and no materials were brought from any distance. While the cube design is based on simplicity, strength, and inexpensive materials and methods, it also has a handsome, if probably unintended, abstract quality—like a minimalist sculpture or even a giant frame— so that looking through the cube is like looking at a painting of the land. The observation deck also offers shelter from the weather and is thus a gesture of hospitality to visitors.

This tower is set in an open, agricultural landscape at the top of V´yhon Hill. Like the locust trees that formed it, this beacon is a metaphor for a tree, as its circular profile ensures durability in the face of wind. It is composed of thirty structural pillars that decrease in diameter as they rise. Thinning of the load-bearing frame corresponds to the lowering tension of the material, from the heavily loaded pedestal to a balustrade that bears no load. On the ascent, the view opens little by little, from an almost closed pedestal all the way to the platform at the top. The inner stairway follows the order of the structure, as a console of planks forms each stair. A spatial spiral made of interconnecting consoles reinforces the structure and defines the inner space with an empty core illuminated from above.

Tower in a Field

AL BORDE ARQUITECTOS / MACHACHI, ECUADOR

The Norwegian Wild Reindeer Pavilion is situated in the Dovrefjell Mountains, home to Europe's last wild reindeer herds and the natural habitat for many rare plants and animals. A mile-long nature path brings visitors to the site, nearly 4,000 feet above sea level.

Since the pavilion is intended to accommodate groups of visitors in a remote and sometimes inhospitable climate, the project required a protective shelter that would allow panoramic views of the landscape without disrupting its natural beauty. The building design is based on a rigid outer shell with an organic inner core. Reminiscent of rock or ice eroded by wind and running water, the south-facing exterior wall and the interior create a protected and warm gathering place, while still preserving the visitor's view of the spectacular natural panorama.

The simple form and natural materials reference local building traditions. The rectangular frame is raw steel resembling the iron ore found in the local bedrock. Over time, the rusted color will blend with the natural colors in the surroundings. Norwegian shipbuilders in Hardangerfjord created the organic forms from 10-inch square pine beams. The wood was then assembled in a traditional way using only wood pegs as fasteners. The exterior wall was treated with pine tar while the interior wood has been oiled.

SNØHETTA
DOVREFJELL NATIONAL PARK, DOVRE, NORWAY

Norwegian Wild Reindeer Pavilion

Aurland Lookout

The site is above Aurland, a small town in Sogn og Fjordane, one of the larger fjords on the west coast of Norway. To make the situation even more dramatic, the lookout creates the experience of leaving the mountainside. The construction creates a distinct horizon: a bridge in the open room of this large fjord. The terrain and the vegetation are protected so that visitors can come out of the landscape and experience it as pristine. All of the large pine trees on the site were preserved, allowing an interaction between the structure and nature. Visitors can walk out into the air through the treetops, helping dramatize the experience of nature and the larger landscape.

SAUNDERS ARCHITECTURE / AURLAND, NORWAY

Set in the riparian forest along the banks of the Mur River, Murturm overlooks the border with Slovenia. Once part of the security zone along the former Iron Curtain, the area became a nature preserve and is now part of the European Green Belt.

Murturm was designed to mark the Green Belt biotope compound system and to serve as an observation tower. Its steel and aluminum-clad double helix design makes it a piece of architectural sculpture. The climb up the intertwining, double-staircase involves not only the elation of having reached the top, but the experience and enjoyment of the stages along the way there. Although completely contemporary in its materials, the observation tower fits into the landscape as a sympathetic counterpoint.

The supporting structure is designed like a tree. The lower part corresponds with the trunk, whereas the tubular steel structure represents the more delicate branches above. Visitors climbing the stairs feel the building gently sway. Depending on the weather and time of day, the wonderful gleam of the aluminum balustrade and the play of light on the shiny surfaces changes the tower's appearance.

Murturm

TERRAIN:LOENHART&MAYR / GOSDORF, STYRIA, AUSTRIA

STUDIOS, PERFORMANCE SPACES, AND SITE-SPECIFIC SCULPTURE INTEGRATE ART AND NATURE.   **ART**

Built on an inaccessible site at an elevation of 3,500 meters, the Atelier Greenhouse accommodates a couple who work in the midst of nature. This is a place of inspiration and meditation for him — a safe vantage point from which to observe and paint the surrounding landscape. For her, the atelier is a pedestal for her greenhouse, a place where she can contemplate the endless landscape and collect its flora.

The atelier sits on a stone base, reaching toward the vegetation of the greenhouse and the sky beyond and suspended between stone walls and ones of rammed earth. The first rays of the sun heat a radiator system that raises the temperature in the gap between the walls. This heated air enters and warms the workspace. In the afternoon, the main facade absorbs the sun's heat, storing it in the floor of the workshop and releasing it during the night. Given the difficulty of reaching the site, it was decided to use indigenous materials: earth, stone, pine, and eucalyptus.

Atelier Greenhouse

AL BORDE ARQUITECTOS / MACHACHI, ECUADOR

ALICE STUDIO, ECOLE POLYTECHNIQUE FEDERALE DE LAUSANNE
LAKE STELLI, NEAR ZERMATT, SWITZERLAND

Evolver

Evolver is a sculpture erected for the Zermatt Festival, an annual chamber music event featuring the Berlin Philharmonic. As an architectural artifact, Evolver intervenes spatially on the panorama surrounding Zermatt. To take full advantage of the views, the project sits next to Lake Stelli, at an altitude of 2,536 meters. The structure consists of a succession of twenty-four rotating frames supporting an enclosed space. As visitors progress through the space, a concealed but uninterrupted 720-degree movement unravels along a transformed panorama. This transformation occurs as people move through a series of openings, only to be caught in a sequence of unexpected views from the original landscape.

Developed as a legacy project for the celebration of Highland culture, Outlandia is an artist's field station that allows and encourages creative interaction between artists and the land, its history and its people. Because of proximity and interaction with the modern tourist trade, Outlandia is in dense woods, reachable by a small path, although it does have a big view across the glen. The artists occupy a cabin in the woods, where they can explore the authenticity of mediated experience and experience of place.

Inspiration for the artist's retreat came from childhood dens, wildlife hides, and bothies, from forest outlaws and Japanese poetry platforms. On the ground, the choice of site grew out of long crawls through wet undergrowth and up wooded slopes, in clouds of midges and carpets of pine needles, in search of natural and human drama. The building itself juts out from a 45-degree slope, entered across a bridge from the slope behind. It is a simple box, leaning out into the view with large windows. Part of the construction was a low-impact, eco-friendly use of material recovered from the site; part was the opposite, high-impact landings for concrete foundations from a helicopter. Construction was part joinery, part forestry, and part mountain rescue, with a local contractor who combined all three.

Outlandia
Field Station

MALCOLM FRASER ARCHITECTS
GLEN NEVIS, LOCHABER, HIGHLAND, SCOTLAND

Yucca Crater

Yucca Crater is a synthetic earthwork that doubled as a recreational amenity during High Desert Test Sites in October 2011. High Desert Test Sites generates physical and conceptual spaces for art exploring the intersections between contemporary art and life at large. After the weekend event, Yucca Crater was abandoned to the entropic forces of the landscape.

Yucca Crater expanded on concepts borrowed from land art, alluding to the abandoned suburban swimming pools and ramshackle homesteads scattered across the Mojave Desert. The work resembled a basin that measured thirty feet from rim to low point and was sunk ten feet into the earth. Rock climbing holds mounted on the interior allowed visitors to descend into a deep pool of salt water. The rough plywood structure of Yucca Crater was originally the formwork used to construct another Ball-Nogues work, Talus Dome, in which more than nine hundred boulder-sized polished metal spheres were assembled to appear as a monumental pile of gravel. The two projects were "cross-designed" such that the method of production used in the first (Talus Dome) has become the central aesthetic for the second (Yucca Crater).

55/02

55/02 was commissioned by The Kielder Partnership, an organization that has introduced more than twenty works of art and architecture into the Water and Forest Park since 1995. Invited to design "some form of shelter" that "engaged with its surroundings," sixteen*(makers) chose to refer to the region's industrial history and collaborate with Stahlbogen GmbH steel manufacturers to develop the experimental building.

Described as "a manufactured architecture in a manufactured landscape," the structure takes its name from its latitude and longitude. The shelter can be seen in glimpses from afar, but its full impact is not revealed until the visitor arrives at the site through a maze of paths. Constructed from thick folded steel drawn, shaped, and fabricated with painstaking accuracy, this bold red structure is an enigmatic resting point at the tip of a spit of land jutting into the lake. It picks up on the relationships between the verticality of the trees and the horizontality of the water. The smooth bright coloured manufactured nature of the steel makes an easy contrast with the organic mature woodland that surrounds it.

As a deliberately curious and speculative work, 55/02 challenges the boundaries between art, architecture, engineering, and craft, at the same time that it is underpinned by an intimate exchange between the related but all too often independent disciplines of design and building.

SIXTEEN*(MAKERS)
KIELDER WATER AND FOREST PARK, NORTHUMBERLAND, ENGLAND

Dovecote Studio is part of the internationally renowned music campus at Snape Maltings, founded by Benjamin Britten in derelict industrial buildings on the Suffolk coast. Britten was inspired by the almost abstract landscape of the reed beds at the boundary between the land and the sea.

With views out across the marshes, Dovecote Studio occupies the ruins of a nineteenth-century dovecote. It expresses the internal volume of the Victorian structure as a Corten steel "lining," a welded structure that was built next to the ruin and craned in when complete. The building is fully welded in a single piece, like the hull of a ship, to achieve weather tightness, and then fitted with a simple plywood inner lining.

A large roof window provides even north light for artists, while a small mezzanine platform with a writing desk in front of glazed corner window offers writers long views over the marshes towards the sea. The single volume will be used by artists-in-residence, by musicians as rehearsal or performance space (there is a large opening door to an adjoining courtyard), by staff for meetings, or as a temporary exhibition space.

Only the minimum necessary brickwork repairs were carried out to stabilize the existing ruin prior to inserting the new structure. Decaying windows were left alone and vegetation growing over the dovecote was protected to allow it to continue a natural process of aging and decay.

The Corten structure itself is fabricated from full size sheets with regular staggered welded joints, into which door and window openings are inserted as required by the internal layout. The interior walls and ceiling are insulated, sealed with a high-performance vapor control layer, and lined with spruce plywood to create a timber "box" within the Corten shell.

HAWORTH TOMPKINS
SNAPE MALTINGS, SNAPE, SUFFOLK, UNITED KINGDOM

Dovecote Studio

The structure, a 150-year-old tobacco barn on a fourth-generation family farm, is romantically named "Far Shed" because it sits alone in the field, remote from the main house.

Shedding Light offered the opportunity to appreciate the utilitarian tobacco shed re-contextualized as art. Built for the purpose of drying harvested tobacco leaves, these sheds represent a significant regional agricultural vernacular, yet the barns are disappearing from the landscape. The challenge here was to use public art to draw attention to the physical and cultural landscapes that surround the farm, while raising their profile in the regional consciousness.

The proposal for this installation was relatively simple: fill the aging tobacco shed interior with lights, open the vertical ventilation panels and allow the light to spill out onto the fields to create a lantern in the landscape during the darkest month of the year. Both the material and immaterial were engaged in this project, as light itself became part of the landscape. This illumination highlighted both the physical architecture of the shed as well as perspectives towards the landscape that it brightened.

While Shedding Light was a temporary project, photography documented the effects of the illumination in changing light and captured the work in changing weather conditions.

ERIKA ZEKOS / AMHERST, MASSACHUSETTS

Shedding Light

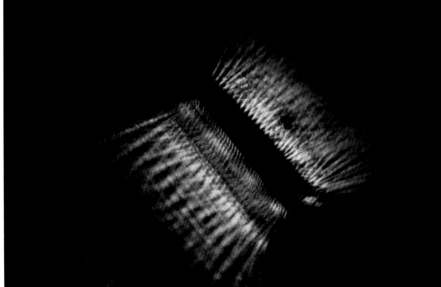

Sandworm is an organic structure/
space/creature realized on the
tidal dunes of the Wenduine coast-
line. Constructed entirely out of
willow, the space is intended for
picnics, relaxation, and postindustrial
meditation.

Marco Casagrande describes
the piece as "weak architecture,"
a human-made structure that wishes
to become part of nature through
flexibility and organic presence.

CASAGRANDE LABORATORY / WENDUINE, BELGIUM

Sandworm

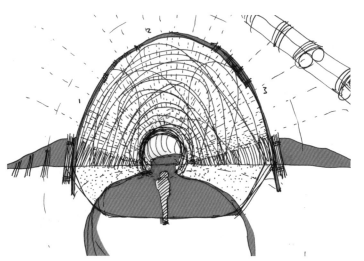 

OPEN TO THE SKY OR CLOSE TO THE EARTH, THESE ARE PLACES OF SOLACE AND REPOSE.

MEDITATION

River Tower and Studio / Chapel of the Sky

This is a remote site in the Colorado mountains overlooking the upper Arkansas River. The Ute people hunted and camped along the river, and during the gold rush of the 1870s, miners' cabins and a stagecoach blacksmith shop defined the architecture. The current owner, an architect, designed and built two log cabins as a family retreat in 1983. The main cabin and guest cabin have outside decks and doors that bring the sound of the river indoors. A tower provides a high, secluded perch for meditation and reading, and captures views of the surrounding peaks, the river, and eagles and hawks that nest in the rock cliffs. The chapel is the final addition to the family "village," a place for reflection on life, nature, and the surrounding environment. Standing alone atop a rock outcropping, this simple wooden form is perched on legs as a reminder that the structure is a privileged visitor within the landscape and treads lightly to minimize its impact. Inside a dramatic stair fills the space and directs the view to the sky through a massive window at the top of an elevated platform.

RON MASON, ANDERSON MASON DALE ARCHITECTS IN COLLABORATION WITH KIEL MOE
GRANITE, COLORADO

A clearing in a quiet area, replete with flora and fauna, near the north bank of the Rio Salado was selected for the Tumbleweed Bower. Easily accessed on foot or by bicycle, it also provided a ready supply of dry tumbleweeds.

The idea was to create a temporary space constructed from the Arizona landscape, a structure built with a network of branches and thorns. The designer's childhood play often included making sculptures from debris and objects found in the landscape. The shelters

Tumbleweed Bower

MAYME KRATZ STUDIO WITH TEAM TUMBLEWEED
RIO SALADO, PHOENIX, ARIZONA

became safe places, providing freedom to read, write poetry, sing, daydream, and imagine.

Tumbleweeds were collected in this hot dusty landscape with the intent of building a shelter that evoked those childhood efforts. Beneath the thistles was debris, bits of plastic, cans, knives, credit cards, and other colorful objects. These walls reveal fragile eco-systems, strange beauty — insights in detritus. During the process of gathering, bowerbirds came to

mind. Amazing architects and foragers, the male birds collect brightly colored objects and create elaborate displays within their nests, all in an effort to attract a mate. The Tumbleweed Bower became an intricate nest and the chandelier within, homage to these lovely, strange birds.

MICHAEL VAN VALKENBURGH ARCHITECTS
MARTHA'S VINEYARD, MASSACHUSETTS

Krakow
Ice Garden

Built as part of a private residence, the Ice Garden celebrates seasonal aspects of the dramatic shorefront environment of Martha's Vineyard. Dappled, semi-transparent, and translucent light is created by profusion of leafy vines or the gradual drips of frozen water that fill the framework of the curved mesh screen at different times of the year. Beginning in spring, purple clematis bloom on the circle of steel mesh, followed by blue morning glory in summer, and the red of Boston ivy in autumn. In the winter, a drip irrigation system feeds formation of ice on the scrim. Within the circle are raised French planting beds.

Field Chapel

ILLINOIS INSTITUTE OF TECHNOLOGY / BOEDIGHEIM, GERMANY

The chapel was designed for an ecumenical church cooperative in the Odenwald-Bauland, a rural region in northern Baden-Württemberg. The chapel stands on a high point, in the hilly fields between the villages of Bödigheim, Seckach, and Großeicholzheim, a site that can only be reached on foot or by bicycle.

The task of the design was to create a place of spirituality—"an interdenominational chapel, a space for people to commune with their God, a place for quiet reflection or simple meditation, but also one that welcomes hikers and cyclists who appreciate a beautiful rest stop." The chapel was built through the cooperative efforts of IIT students, the minister, the blacksmith, the carpenter, the sawmill owners, and the farmer who owns the field. The chapel was built of wood harvested locally, and all materials and labor were donated and sourced nearby.

The chapel, with its window-less tower, is reached along a narrow footpath and is set in a gravel forecourt bounded on two sides by massive limestone benches. A brick platform leads visitors to the first "room," open to the sky above. The sanctuary is the same size, but the upward view is the interior the tower. Horizontal wood slates with large spaces in between admit light (not unlike regional tobacco barns), creating a remarkable play of light and shadow as visitors move around the building. Visible from afar, the chapel is a landmark on the horizon.

MOORHEAD & MOORHEAD IN COLLABORATION WITH RICHARD MOORHEAD
BASED IN FARGO, NORTH DAKOTA

Mobile Chaplet

Mobile Chaplet is one of six portable spaces for reflection commissioned to travel to rural communities around the state of North Dakota as part of the Roberts Street Chaplet Project.

The conceptual starting points for the Mobile Chaplet were the covered wagons that transported settlers to the Midwest, as well as the vaulted forms of traditional church naves. The design itself is the result of countless study models that explored the range of forms that could be created by weaving a series of rods of identical length (the form comes from variations in the distance spanned by each rod).

The final pattern consists of two vaulted forms, one nested inside the other. Weaving was chosen as a method of construction, in part because it allowed for a space that is simultaneously intimate and open to the surrounding prairie land-scape. It also reflected the linear nature of the paintings of the artist who commissioned the Chaplet and painted a mural on its floor. Constructed on a trailer bed, the vaulted canopy is composed of over 200 thirty-foot long thermoplastic composite rods. A bench floats above the trailer bed supported by the rods that also act as a backrest for the bench.

The Floating Sauna is a gift to the Rosendal community, a village at the end of the majestic Hardangerfjord in Norway. The sauna celebrates the ancient but still living connection between the human built environment and the great voice of the ocean. The Viking descendant Rosendal villagers are as natural with house building as with ship building, and the Floating Sauna lies somewhere in between.

Reached by swimming or by rowing a boat, the sauna sits on a raft anchored to the sea floor, Inside the temperature can rise to 80 degrees, but the cool ocean is just one step away. The hot sauna moves and rocks according to the mood of the sea.

The walls are semi-transparent showing silhouettes of those inside. While sitting inside the sea literally feels as though it is flowing in, and the modern man is cleansed by nature.

CASAGRANDE LABORATORY / ROSENDAL VILLAGE, HARDANGERFJORD, NORWAY

Floating Sauna

RESTING PLACES ON THE JOURNEY THROUGH MOUNTAINS, FOREST, AND OPEN FIELDS.

SHELTER

The HemLoft

JOEL ALLEN / WHISTLER MOUNTAIN, BRITISH COLUMBIA

The Hemloft hangs in a mature stand of hemlocks on a precipitous slope about five minutes walk from the nearest road. The intent was to build a compact forest cabin on a minimal budget that would mesh elegantly with its environment and age gracefully with use.

The idea of a treehouse was appealing because of its minimal footprint and its tidy orientation about the forest floor. The egg-shaped orb was chosen because the structure could be contained within its form: eight curved ribs connect to the tree at the top. The floor intersects the ribs two-thirds of the way down from the top to form a stable three-pointed frame.

The final design comprises an entry nook, a desk area, and an outdoor covered kitchen, accessed through a sliding glass pocket door. Spiral stairs wind around the tree to a loft with four hatches that open to the treetops.

Winnipeg is a city of 600,000 residents located on the Canadian prairie. It is the coldest city of its size outside of Siberia. The Red and the Assiniboine Rivers meet in the center of the city. In winter, after the snow is plowed, residents can enjoy skating trails that extend for many miles. With temperatures that drop to minus 30 and 40 dgrees celsius for long periods of time, and winds that can make minus 30 feel like minus 50, creating shelter from the wind greatly enhances the possibility of using the river skating trails.

These intimate shelters, each accommodating only a few people at a time, stand with their backs to the wind like buffalo, seeming to have life and purpose as they huddle together, shielding each other from the elements. Each shelter is formed of thin, flexible plywood that is given both structure and spatial character through bending and deformation. Skins, made of two layers of flexible plywood, are cut in patterns and attached to a timber armature that consists of a triangular base and wedge-shaped spine and ridge members.

Grouping the shelters into a cluster begins with the relationship of two, and their juxtaposition to qualify the size and accessibility of their entrance openings. This apparently casual pairing is actually achieved by a precise rotation. Three pairs (one with mirror reflection) are then placed in relation to one another through a secondary rotation to form the cluster and define an intermediate 'interior' space within the larger grouping. Together, the shelters create dynamic solar/wind relationships that shift according to specific orientation, time and environmental circumstance.

These are delicate and "alive" structures. They move gently in the wind, creaking and swaying to and fro at various frequencies, floating precariously on the surface of the frozen river, shaking off any snow that might adhere to their surfaces. Their fragile and tenuous nature makes those sheltered by them supremely aware of the inevitability, ferocity, and beauty of winter on the Canadian prairies.

PATKAU ARCHITECTS / WINNIPEG, MANITOBA, CANADA

Skating Shelters

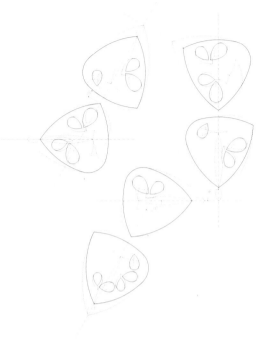

The pavilion is set in the new growth Da Nong Da Fu Forest and Eco-park in Hualien province, Taiwan. Used for sugarcane cultivation under Japanese rule, Hualien is the traditional territory of the aboriginal Taiwanese Amis tribe, but it is now in the hands of the Taiwanese government. The project was conceived within the context of an art festival curated by Huichen Wu of Artfield, Taipei, for Taiwan's Forestry Bureau to raise public awareness of a new growth forest threatened by development.

The Forest Pavilion serves as a shaded meeting and performance space and as the primary venue for the festival's opening and closing ceremonies. This new circular gathering space emerges from the ground in a series of eleven green-bamboo shading vaults, organized in two rings around a void. The plan is inspired by the rings of a tree, and the different forms of the vaults by growth patterns in nature. The pavilion sits lightly in its environment with minimal disruption, yet with lighting, it becomes a beacon at night, underscoring the relative emptiness of the valley.

Using techniques developed by nArchitects for the 2004 Canopy for MoMA P.S.1, the indigenous Amis tribe undertook freshly cut green bamboo fabrication for the pavilion. Through an exchange of knowledge and ideas about bamboo construction, the Amis became personally invested in the pavilion, naming it Y lu duqai a luma, Amis for "mountain home."

nARCHITECTS / GUANGFU, HUALIEN, TAIWAN

Forest Pavilion

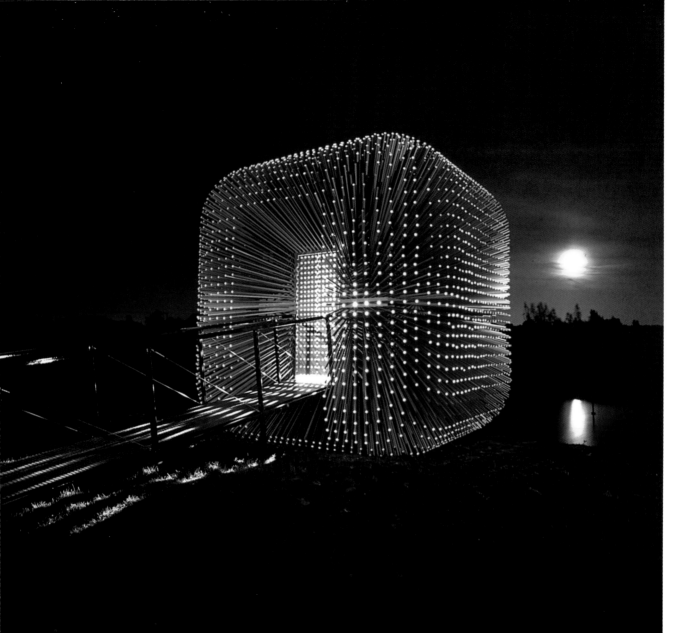

Sitooterie II

The National Malus (crab-apple) Collection commissioned Heatherwick to design a permanent pavilion to sit within their grounds. The structure takes its name from the Scottish word for small building. The cube is 2.4 meters in each dimension, and it is punctured by more than 5,000 square, hollow aluminium rods with tiny glased ends that act as miniature windows. The rods form the structure and texture of the building and lift the cube one meter above the ground. They are arranged radially, emanating from the center of the cube. A single light source at this central point emits light at night through every tube, causing the windows to glow. Seating is created by elements that extend into the cube to support a machined aluminium surface.

HEATHERWICK STUDIO
BARNARD'S FARM, WEST HORNDON, ESSEX, UNITED KINGDOM

Shadow Pavilion

The Matthaei Botanical Garden at the University of Michigan is a hands-on community laboratory for conserving, restoring, and celebrating the environment. Located between the main entrance drive and an education path that overlooks a landscape under restoration as a prairie, the Shadow Pavilion functions both as a landmark along an educational walking circuit and as a contemplative space to observe, hear, and experience the landscape.

A lightweight, self-supporting structure made from thin gauge aluminum sheet metal, the structure is an assembly of aluminum cones informed by the biological principles of phyllotaxis. The cones funnel sound, light, and precipitation to the interior intensifying the visual and acoustic qualities of being in the landscape.

PLY ARCHITECTURE / ANN ARBOR, MICHIGAN

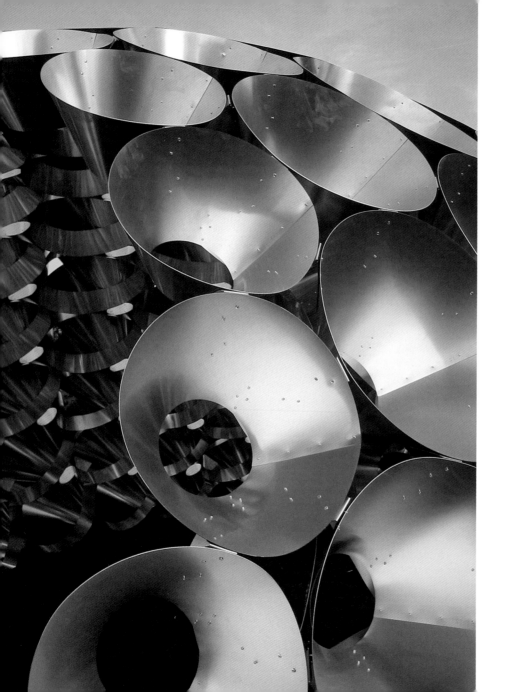

Middenin

Originally a dairy farm, the property called de kleine Wildenberg now functions as a place for care of the disabled and elderly. The yard is full of barns, houses, and activity, but the rural surrounding is unique, a combination of nature and agriculture close to the Hanseatic city of Deventer.

In the middle of a meadow is a serene place that serves as a resting point for walkers and cyclists and also as a drinking and sheltering place for cattle. The land is part of a recreational network of local farms and gardens, where visitors can rest and enjoy the hospitality. Middenen is one of a series of functional artworks commissioned by Kunstenlab Deventer for these local resting points.

The shelter celebrates arrival on the farm, the walk through the meadow, and the perfect stay in the middle of the landscape. Together with the animals, both visitors and farmers can find pure contact with their surroundings. The access to the meadow is an essential part of the work. The area (and particularly this family farm) is famous for its hospitality, but the farmers do not allow access to the heart of private meadows and roads, which forms the real character of the area. This contradiction was the starting point for the work.

Middenin consists of a basic steel construction of L-beams, filled in with a patchwork of materials from the farm. The prepared pieces of steel were welded together on site. Together with visitors to the area, the architects constructed the facades, floor, roof, and windows from materials found on the farm.

OBSERVATORIUM
DIEPENVEEN, NEAR DEVENTER, OVERIJSSEL, THE NETHERLANDS

met de fiets op(de) weg

RUST

PUNT

An integral part of the education of Taliesin apprentices is designing and building their own sleeping quarters for their use during their tenure as students.

With a simple gesture, the Hook Shelter lifts the student above the ground with enough room for a shaded bed platform. Desert Perch is an adaptation of a 1960s shelter that was stripped to the bare masonry and superimposed with a skeleton of lightweight steel channels clad with polycarbonate. The detailing clearly differentiates the old structure from the new, and its upright posture allows a cantilevered sleeping perch to the northeast and a living-study area. Raising the basic sheepherder's tent off the ground, the designers of Hanging Tent Shelter turned the tent form into a suspended platform with the sweeping views in all directions and protection from desert animals. The tent roof was recently replaced with intricately faceted polycarbonate panels.

FRANK LLOYD WRIGHT/TALIESIN FELLOWSHIP
TALIESIN WEST, SCOTTSDALE, ARIZONA

Hook Shelter / Desert Perch Shelter / Hanging Tent Shelter

There are seven Landmarks along ancient trails through the coastal mountain range that runs along the Pacific Ocean toward the Central Valley in Chile. Marking route changes or the junction with an intersecting path, these structures serve both as objects for orientation along the trail and as resting areas for tourists. They are also designed to act as public space — meeting points for the outsider and residents. The design and building of these signs reflects the interest of the architecture students in connecting to this region, known as the Dry Lands, which has not seen many benefits of modernity and whose young people often leave in search of work.

The Landmarks were built with scrap wood left over from the local forest industry. Each of the seven is a different design, based on the size of the pieces of wood that are shaped and glued. These labor-intensive wooden canvases are true signposts or markers — literally landmarks — for the specific locales and meeting places and have given them an identity. The seating shaped from the wood is innovative, creating objects of curiosity and visual interest.

Landmark

UNIVERSITY OF TALCA / MACHACHI, CHILE

Designed for the Schuylkill Center for Environmental Education, RainShelter is a prototype that can be easily and inexpensively replicated. Constructed of post-consumer recyclable materials, RainShelter is designed to act as a musical fountain in the rain, as a kaleidoscopic light show in bright sunlight, and as a whistle in the wind.

RainShelter not only offers protection from the elements, but it also allows interaction with those elements. This combination umbrella and "primitive hut" is both utilitarian and poetic. Large enough for four people to sleep in, RainShelter is constructed like a geometrical puzzle that engages rain, sun, and wind.

A pyramidal structure where engineered wood panels (OSB) act like a skin that both sheds rain and allows bright light to enter. The panels are of a single manufactured size, easy to transport and to attach; they circle the central axis and get smaller as they ascend toward to the top. A play area at the base is made of rubber chips produced from recycled tires— a rubber mulch that is non-toxic and non-staining. Once built, the shelter assumes a more whimsical role. Designed as delight for the senses, here one can listen to the musical rain drops falling, smell the humidity of the soil, hear the wind whistle, and feel the power of the sun.

RainShelter

GABRIELA SANZ RODRIGUEZ AND CARLOS MARTINEZ-MEDIERO
PHILADELPHIA, PENNSYLVANIA

EXPLORING, PROTECTING, AND HARNESSING THE NATURAL WORLD.   **WORKING**

Perry Lakes Park Covered Bridge

Perry Lakes Park, on the outskirts of Marion, Alabama, lies along the shores of the Cahaba River. The park features four oxbow lakes, formed over many years by the meandering waters of the river, which create a distinct swampland ecotone characterized by Spanish moss and cypress trees.

An oxbow lake and inlet stream rendered the east side of the park inaccessible. By placing a footbridge across the inlet stream, visitors could gain access to the oxbow lakes and a wider array of hiking trails that explore the area's rich ecological diversity. The addition of a bridge also opened the possibility of a birding tower adjacent to the oxbow lake.

The form of the bridge refers to the vernacular covered bridges once commonplace in rural Alabama. The cypress lumber and weathering steel structure maintain visual continuity with the surrounding environment. The structure consists of two leaning trusses making up the asymmetrical roof, with a third horizontal truss completing the structural triangle. The truss rests on two columns located at the fulcrum points. A walkway suspended from the truss creates a floating path below.

The Urban Farm at Stapleton is the largest 4H program in Colorado. On twenty-three acres, this education center serves more than four thousand children a year by introducing and engaging them with livestock and guinea fowl. Their mission is to improve the lives of children living in high-risk, urban neighborhoods by instilling a sense of positive self-regard, a strong work ethic, and hope.

The Learning Cube marks the entry to the Urban Farm as an open-air pavilion and market. Built with walls and ceilings of re-purposed wooden pallets and lumber reclaimed from a demolished railroad bridge, the Learning Cube is a sustainable, shaded outdoor gathering space, market, and classroom.

The Dairy House is a hands-on training facility, designed as a model for urban farming. In particular, Dairy House demonstrates the essentials of dairy goat farming by integrating the animal pen with an easy access platform and a goat stanchion to assist in shearing and milking. The structure provides relief from the elements as its gabion cage walls buffer the western sun, its north wall tempers the prevailing winds, and its large roof offers shade to the students and workers.

STUDIO H:T / UNIVERSITY OF COLORADO DENVER
DESIGN BUILD STUDIO
DENVER, COLORADO

The Learning Cube and Dairy House

Chicken Chapel

MOSKOW LINN ARCHITECTS — STUDIO NORTH / NORWICH, VERMONT

Located on a 117-acre farm consisting of woodlands, open fields, stream, and ponds, the Chicken Chapel sits in a small paddock adjacent to a wood and stone barn. Designed as a light-filled, airy environment for raising chickens and/or other feathered livestock, the chapel is constructed of sugar maple poles sustainably harvested from the site and a fiberglass roof. The wood frame is lined with translucent fiberglass that admits light and warmth and protects from the elements. The whole structure can be prefabricated and easily replicated.

The chicken chapel is a single space for a growing flock. A human-scaled door on the north provides access for servicing the coop, and a chicken-scaled door on the south allows the birds to free range. A nesting box creates a secondary enclosure where the chickens build nests and lay eggs. A multi-level roost allows for additional feathered livestock to cohabitate in the structure. Diffuse light creates an ever-changing environment. In the evening the structure glows like a Japanese lantern.

Bat Tower

Griffis Sculpture Park is a 450-acre park located approximately forty miles south of Buffalo and eight miles north of Ellicottville. The park features more than 250 large-scale sculptures, sited within a landscape of varying terrain, vegetation, and miles of hiking trails.

Bat Tower is a bat habitation prototype that explores strategies for increasing public awareness of bats as a critical component of our ecosystem. Bats are effective as natural pesticides, pollinators, and mosquito abatement. Yet they are often considered as a kind of urban pest and are frequently exterminated. Their very survival is also being challenged by White Nose Syndrome, a disease that has been wiping out large bat populations in the northeastern United States.

Bat Tower challenges notions of the typical off-the-shelf bat house. Rather than innocuously fading into the background, the tower stands as a prominently visible outdoor sculpture. Drawing from the idea of a vertical cave, the installation has a heavy and intense presence, contrasting the lightness and invisibility associated with do-it-yourself bat house constructions.

Bat Tower is sited and designed to facilitate bat inhabitation. Located adjacent to a pond, the site boasts an abundance of mosquitoes and other bat-attracting insects. Chives, oregano, and other bat-attracting herbs are planted within the base of the tower. To help entry, the project's ribbed construction includes a series of 'landing pads' near the top of the tower. A pattern of grooves on both vertical and horizontal surfaces allows bats to climb more easily into the tower and cling to its "ceilings." To provide warm interior for bat roosting, dark wood panels cover the tower's inhabitation zone in order to absorb sunlight.

ANTS OF THE PRAIRIE
GRIFFIS SCULPTURE PARK, ASHFORD HOLLOW FOUNDATION, EAST OTTO, NEW YORK

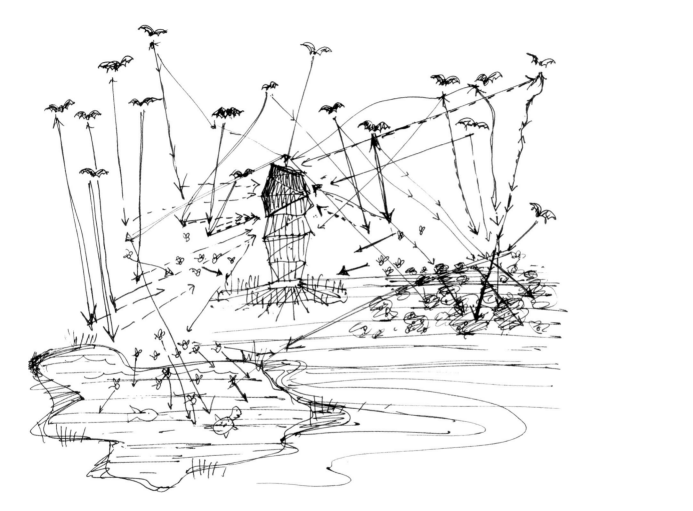

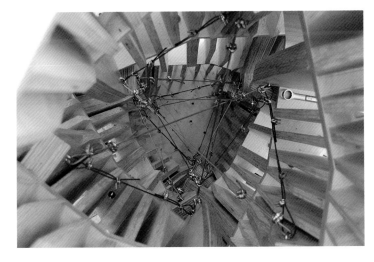

The Ghost 9 barn can be viewed as a landscape interpretation instrument. Its pure tubular form tilts in response to the undulating agrarian landscape. The floating wood tube is anchored to the ground by the tractor shed and combines with adjacent structures to create barnyard microclimates.

The larger tube component functions as a "loafing barn," sheltering horses and sheep from sun, wind, and rain. The grounding "tractor box" is used for storing equipment and hay storage, as well as sheep stalls.

The choice of building materials was, in part, driven by the extremely aggressive schedule: the building was designed in one week and constructed in five days in collaboration with Ghost Laboratory participants. Foundations are treated telephone poles, like a traditional pole barn. All lumber is relatively rot-resistant hemlock, custom-milled by a local sawmill, to ensure easy materials access, and requiring only basic carpentry skills. The most significant structural challenge involved transferring lateral wind loads into the ground, given the floating form in the landscape.

Ghost 9

MACKAY-LYONS SWEETAPPLE ARCHITECTS / NOVA SCOTIA, CANADA

Drumlin Farm Wildlife Sanctuary is a working farm and wildlife sanctuary operated by the Massachusetts Audubon Society. The outdoor classroom, supporting a summer camp program for fifth and sixth graders, sits in a wooded site adjacent to the primary farmland.

Built with red pine harvested from surrounding forest, the classroom is set into a natural clearing at the intersection of existing paths. It was designed to blend with its surroundings while simultaneously communicating its purpose. The canopy serves as a beacon, easily visible upon approach along the pathways. Yet it projects the play of light and shadow through the pine boughs and oak leaves of the surrounding trees onto the canopy. The built project itself is a learning tool for summer camp students, teaching them how wood, concrete, and steel interact to create structure and interact with the rural setting.

Drumlin Farm Outdoor Classroom

DESIGNLAB ARCHITECTS / LINCOLN, MASSACHUSETTS

The barn at Fallingwater was originally a bank barn for a nineteenth-century farmstead. The farmhouse and a springhouse also remain. The land immediately around the barn is in pasture, but significant nearby swaths were reforested late in the twentieth century.

The first step in renovating the barn for use as office, exhibit, and event space was removing the large colony of brown bats from their residence in the ridge of the roof and transferring them to other quarters.

The bat house is constructed of multiple vertical layers of roughly textured plywood, spaced to create narrow slots for the bats to crawl up to resting spaces at the ridge of the structure. The layers are flaked at the bottom to provide landing platforms for each of the slots. A roof keeps the rain out. The structure is dark colored and faces

south to soak up warmth from the sun. The bat house is located high above the ground in the pasture, about thirty feet from the edge of the woods, making it convenient to bat hunting grounds along the edge of the forest. In recognition of Gothic associations with bats, the bat house has absorbed a medieval flavor.

Bat House for the Barn at Fallingwater

BOHLIN CYWINSKI JACKSON / MILL RUN, PENNSYLVANIA

June Moore is a beekeeper. The prized sourwood honey produced by the bees in her beehives is sold along country roads and at local markets. In 1998 June wanted to add two structures, an apiarian structure for processing and storing honey and a carport/outdoor work area.

The Honey House is a modern four-sided hive box organized as a series of shallow orthogonal frames that articulate and separate the brood chamber below from the "super" (honey chamber) above. Moveable frames allow the stored comb honey to be removed without upsetting the brood chamber. While the Cartesian frames delimit the space of bee activity and make it manageable, they have virtually no effect on the constructed organic patterns of the bee colony's day-to-day activities. The tense interplay between the efficiency of the beekeeper's equipment and the bee's willingness to adapt to it is central to the continual production of honey and the survival of the colony.

The single most prominent and complex architectural element is a unique load-bearing steel plate and faceted glass wall that acts to organize the storage and display of honey, filter natural light, and provide a rich mosaic of reflections of the surrounding foliage. The multiple spatial configurations within the wall may be transparent, translucent, or opaque, depending upon one's perspective, the season of the year, and the time of day.

MARLON BLACKWELL ARCHITECT / CASHIERS, NORTH CAROLINA

Moore Honey House

Elkhorn River Research Station

One of seven "river probes" located on each of the major rivers in Nebraska, this research station monitors water quality in the Elkhorn River.

All major Nebraska cities are located along the rivers and pump river water into water treatment plants to creat city water. Pollution from factoreis, urban encroachment, agricultural practices, and beef feedlots is compromising the water quality.

Commissioned by the University of Nebraska Aquatic Toxicology Laboratory, the river probes are intended to allow scientists to live on the rivers and conduct long-term ecological monitoring of the surface quality of the water. The probes will also serve as public observation platforms both to view the natural beauty of the river and to learn about the toxicology and pollution issues.

IN THE DESERT, BY THE WATER'S EDGE, REMOTE BUT ENVELOPED BY NATURE.

DWELLING

Flake House

Designed as part of the "Petites machines à habiter" competition, Flake House was displayed in 2009 at the Festival Estuaire Nantes Saint Nazaire at Frossay near the mouth of the Loire River.

Flake House evokes associations of a broken branch. The two parts of the building, three and six meters long respectively, contain a functional area and a living area. They are arranged at an angle, creating a welcoming space between. The building envelope is made of untreated maritime pine tree trunks, with the gable sides covered in wooden disks that simulate stacked wood. The far end of each structure is fully glazed, providing views into and out of the structures.

At two and one-half meters in width, Flake Hoouse has been designed for transportation by truck. At each destination, a mobile crane places them on wooden planks positioned at a 90-degree angle to each other. No other foundation is necessary, making it easy to set up, dismantle, and transport the buildings.

Jerry and Eba Sohn asked Arata Isozaki to design two outdoor sleeping rooms where their family could spend nights under the stars, yet be safe from rattlesnakes. The site is off the grid, up a dirt road in the Mojave Desert, ten miles north of Joshua Tree National Park.

Isozaki designed three outdoor rooms, each nine by nine feet and cast in concrete, based on the four seasons. The winter room is fully enclosed with glazed openings, including a panel set on the roof and Nylint Truck, a mural

Obscured Horizon

by Jeremy Dickinson on the wall. The summer room is a concrete platform balanced on a vertical wall that serves as a place to sleep at night and to meditate during the day. Down the hill is the spring and fall room, where a roof protects from dew and light rain and shades the space. Obscured Horizon by Lawrence Weiner is painted in yellow and orange letters on the exterior wall. All three rooms remind us how delicate our relationship is to both nature and our planet.

Treehouse

ROBERT POTOKAR / TRNOVO, LJUBLJANA, SLOVENIA

This freestanding treehouse can be erected anywhere. Where older trees cannot support the additional weight of a traditional treehouse, this multi-purpose wooden play structure is a stand-alone construction, which can be erected near or around a tree.

This treehouse, conceived with contemporary design principles, is not modelled on any of the classic forms that take their inspiration from either real houses or garden sheds. Instead, children are offered a different understanding of shapes, new spatial experiences, and new forms of play.

The house is made of spruce plywood, protected on the exterior by a colorless nano-varnish. The roof is covered in a roofing paper that shields against most unfavorable weather conditions.

Rolling Huts

The Rolling Huts sit lightly on the site, a flood-plain meadow in a river valley. The owner purchased the site, formerly a RV campground, with the aim of allowing the landscape to return to its natural state. Wheels lift the structures above the meadow, providing an unobstructed view into nature and the surrounding mountains.

Designed to house visitors, each hut is, in essence, an offset, steel-clad box on a steel and wood platform. Walls are topped by clerestory windows, over which a paneled roof floats in a lopsided V. At the north end a double-paned sliding glass door opens to the outside. Interior finishes—cork and plywood—are simple, inexpensive, and left as raw as possible. Exteriors are constructed of durable, no-maintenance materials: steel, plywood, and car-decking.

The huts are grouped as a herd: while each is sited toward a view of the mountains (and away from the other structures), their proximity unites them. Showers, as well as parking, are located in and near the centrally located barn, set a short distance from the herd. Rain run-off and snow-melt from each hut are allowed to percolate into the surrounding naturalized landscape.

OLSON KUNDIG ARCHITECTS
METHOW VALLEY, WASHINGTON

LUKASZ KOS FOUR O NINE / LAKE MUSKOKA, CANADA

Part of a family compound on a peninsula on Lake Muskoka, 4treehouse was designed as a retreat from the main house and guest cottages. Four trees are wrapped in a lattice-like skin, and the interior space is divided into three levels, each offering a different spatial experience. The skin acts like a tree canopy, filtering sunlight in the interior spaces. At night the tree house takes on a cocoon-like quality, becoming a lantern suspended in the forest.

The natural setting demanded ecological sensitivity in order to preserve the trees' health and growth. The traditional Muskoka balloon frame was integrated with innovative engineering so that only one steel cable was attached to each tree, with minimal impact on the growing trunks. From these single attachments, four steel cables (one from each tree) supporting two Douglas fir beams (one for each pair of cables), creating two giant swings on which the Muskoka balloon frame sits.

4treehouse

In the midst of a ten-acre swamp restricted by wetlands and setbacks, the Swamp Hut sits lightly upon the land. Four huts surround a central deck creating a protective enclosure.

Positioned to the north, the cleansing hut, housing the bathroom and kitchette, is the most enclosed. Water is preheated by solar panel and the toilet is composting. Photovoltaics create electricity. Sleeping huts to the east and west have translucent roofs that filter morning light to gently awaken guests. On the south is the table hut, which is furnished with a refectory table for working, reading, and eating. This hut extends over the swamp and is the best location for observing wildlife. The structure, like an open dory, has no roof and the fauna laps against the sides. In inclement weather, a canvas fly may be rolled down. At the center, the deck functions as an outdoor room with views of the landscape through and around the huts.

MOSKOW LINN ARCHITECTS / NEWTON, MASSACHUSETTS

Swamp Hut

MARLON BLACKWELL ARCHITECT
FAYETTEVILLE, ARKANSAS

Keenan Tower House

As a child, the owner spent many memorable days and nights in a treehouse erected by his grandfather; in homage to those memories, he wanted to build a live-in treehouse. In response, the architects proposed a house among the trees—a structure that would soar through the trees, carving the sky.

The textured bark of hickories and oaks inspired the design of a wooden lattice, made of white-oak fins, which filters and reflects light and establishes a visible datum at the height of the tree canopy. From the front, the lattice appears transparent and displaces weight to the metal skin above. With movement around it, the voids between the oak fins perceptually collapse, providing a sense of solidity that "grounds" the tower. White cladding of horizontal standing-seam steel panels above references industrial and agricultural structures in the landscape beyond. Local creek and river stones cover the ground at the base. Inside, the floor is covered with crushed pecan shells.

The program for living is simple—an interior room for viewing the expansive horizon in all directions and an open-roof exterior room that frames the sky above and the land below. Oriented on the cardinal points, the Tower House intensifies the presence of solar and lunar movements and of seasonal change.

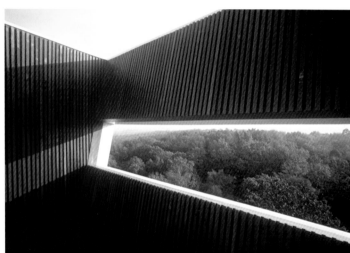

The Signal Shed is within walking distance of the Eagle Cap Wilderness Preserve in northeastern Oregon. The building sits on a steep, heavily wooded site with views of Wallowa Lake, an area that has been revered for its natural beauty since the days of Chief Joseph, legendary leader of the Nez Perce people.

Intended to provide living quarters that access the outdoors, the structure had to connect the interior and exterior when in use, but be secure when left unattended for extended periods of time. To minimize impact on the natural environment and on the surrounding visual landscape, the foundation was built as a series of pier footings. The blackened rain-screen cladding helps the structure recede into the shadows of the surrounding mountains and trees. The "charcoaled" exterior also references the burned trees found onsite and recalls the past use of Signal Mountain as a smoke signal point for the Nez Perce tribe. This mountain (which has been renamed after General Oliver Howard who defeated Chief Joseph) is a backdrop for the primary view from the Signal Shed.

A large sliding door opens the interior space to the outdoors so visitors feel as though they are camping while inside. A single hatch window opens to frame a view of the Wallowa Lake Tramway and Signal Mountain. Windows, which face the forest on the other three elevations, are shuttered by the same slats that wrap the exterior. Inside, a loft, simple wood stove, kitchen counter, and collapsible dining table provide adequate accoutrements for rustic living.

RYAN LINGARD / WALLOWA COUNTY, OREGON

Signal Shed

SAUNDERS ARCHITECTS / HARDANGER FJORD, NORWAY

The site is about two hours drive from Bergen, on the edge of one of Norway's most dramatic fjords. Designed to be at once a part of the natural surroundings and a sensitive contrast to the dramatic landscape, the house is in two parts, one for the eating and sleeping and the other for no specific purpose. A long floating deck connects the two. The front faces the fjords, while the inner space faces the mountain and creates an evening space that can be enhanced by a small fire.

The house is insulated with recycled newspapers, and all the trees on the site have been conserved and integrated into the project. The intention is to have minimalist interiors, with candles as the evening light source. The retreat is approximately 80 meters above sea level, creating a dramatic relationship to the fjord. Nearby are cascading waterfalls.

From the deck the views are hypnotizing. The site has a sacred feeling, with the darker forest in the back and open light at the front.

Summer House

Chen house is on an old Japanese cherry farm near the Datun Volcano in northern Taiwan, where wind, flooding, and heat are major and constant environmental factors.

The house is raised above the ground so that floodwaters run under it. The different spaces are part of a flexible axis of outdoor and indoor functions. The smaller bathroom and kitchen unit acts as a kicker, stabilizing the wooden structure during the frequent typhoons and earthquakes. Attached to the bathroom is a small sauna.

The bio-climatic architecture is designed to catch the cool breeze from the Datun River during hot days, and to let in the light winds circulating on the site between the fresh water reservoir pond and the farmlands. A fireplace is used during the winter for heating and for making tea. The house is not strong or heavy; instead it is weak and flexible. It does not close the environment out, but is designed to give the farmers needed shelter. Ruin is what occurs when the man-made has become part of nature. With this house the architects were looking forward, designing a ruin.

CASAGRANDE LABORATORY / SANJHIH, TAIPEI COUNTY, TAIWAN

Chen House

Contemporary Follies showcases outstanding examples of architectural design that address our place in nature. These works of architecture include places to lounge, live, eat, view, and think. All demonstrate our interconnectedness with the natural world.

Humankind's relationship with nature and the land is one of the most significant tenets of our belief systems. Our attitudes toward nature fundamentally define us. From the beginning of time, attempts to understand our place in the universe have been expressed through works of art and architecture that shape the landscape.

Architecture in and on the landscape is an important artistic aspiration. The examples that make up Contemporary Follies are manifestations of this very long tradition. While the search for an ideal landscape is as old as Eden, these current projects are in the Enlightenment spirit of Jean-Jacques Rousseau and Thomas Jefferson, the English picturesque folly and the forest retreats of the Scandinavian Modernists.

This book features the work of current practitioners and their architecturally significant, small-scale, rural interventions. These latest works make nature more accessible. They allow us to re-interpret the environment and draw us closer to its mysteries.

Keith Moskow
Robert Linn

For Ken Moskow, CIA operative, brother, friend, father, and co-worker who died atop Mt Kilimanjaro in the fall of 2008.

Acknowledgments

Thanks to the all contributors who supplied the material for the book. Without their participation, this publication would not be possible.

Thanks to our associate Zhen Wu, who was the primary book organizer and managed the hundreds of files submitted from around the world.

Thanks to The Monacelli Press and especially our editor, Elizabeth White.

Thanks to Marc Kristal for creating a historical context and to David Blankenship for the elegant layout.

And thanks to our families, including Allison, Erin, Zac, Jake, Jackson, and Ava, who continue to be supportive of our endeavors and, like us, enjoy experiencing follies of today.

Library of Congress Control Number:
2012942290

ISBN: 9781580933407

First edition

10 9 8 7 6 5 4 3 2 1

Designed by David Blankenship / Because
design-because.com

Text set in Replica

The Monacelli Press
236 West 27th Street
New York, New York, 10001

Printed in China

Photography credits

Iwan Baan 196, 198–201
Sam Batchelor 176, 177
Geoffrey D. Beneditto 178, 179, 181
Tom Bies, Olson Kundig Architects 4, 206–210
Randy Brown Architects 186, 188, 189
Casagrande Laboratory 80, 82, 84, 110, 112, 113, 232–37
Albert Chao 168, 170, 171
Cango Chen 124, 126
Florian Claar 127
Fabienne Delafraye 192–95
Diephotodesign 39
James Dow 120, 122, 123
Andrew Flake 98–101
Frank Lloyd Wright/Taliesen Fellowship 142–47
Pascual Gangotena 52, 54, 55, 32–35
Rick Guest 128
Heidi Hermanski and Joel Allen 116–19
Malcolm Fraser Architects 60–63
Brigida Gonzales 102, 104, 105
Villa Hara/HUT Wood Studio 24, 26, 27
Timothy Hursley 22–23
Ketil Jacobsen 36, 40–41
Nathan Jenkins 162, 164, 165
Richard Johnson 182, 184, 185
Chad Kirkpatrick 4, 206–210
Lukasz Kos 212–15
Vesta Kroese, Observatorium 138–41
LAAC Architects 14, 16, 17
Anita Licis-Risak 76, 78 below, 79
Ryan Lingard 224–27
Marc Lins/Hubertus Hamm 46, 48, 49

Brian MacKay Lyons 172, 174, 175
Scott Mayoral 64, 66, 67
Stacey McClure 95, 96, 97
Raymond Meier 197
Adrian Llewelyn Meredith Front cover
Moorhead & Moorhead 106, 108, 109
Moskow Linn Architects 166, 167, 216–19
North Studio at Wesleyan University 22, 23
Frank Ooms Photography 88, 90–93
Ply Architecture 132–37
Robert Potokar 202–205
Christian Richters 18–21
Rural Studio University of Alabama 158, 160, 161
Gabriela Sanz Rodriguez/
Carolos Martinez-Mediero 152–155
Todd Saunders/Saunders Architecture 42, 43, 44, 228–31
Rodrigo Sheward
sixteen*(makers) 68, 70, 71
Steve Speller 130, 131
Jan-Olav Storli 38
Joel Tettamanti/ALICE Studio EPFL 56–59
German Vaelzuela 28, 30
Philip Vile 72–75
University of Talca School of Architecture 148, 150, 151
Erika Zekos 78 top